DATE DUE

GAYLORD — PRINTED IN U.S.A.

D1159710

MIRANDA
COSGROVE

Mitchell Lane
PUBLISHERS

P.O. Box 196
Hockessin, Delaware 19707
Visit us on the web: www.mitchelllane.com
Comments? email us: mitchelllane@mitchelllane.com

CC
JB
17.95
0065

9/08

Mitchell Lane PUBLISHERS

Printing   1   2   3   4   5   6   7   8   9

A Robbie Reader
Contemporary Biography

Albert Pujols	Alex Rodriguez	Aly and AJ
Amanda Bynes	Ashley Tisdale	Brittany Murphy
Charles Schulz	Dakota Fanning	Dale Earnhardt Jr.
Donovan McNabb	Drake Bell & Josh Peck	Dr. Seuss
Dwayne "The Rock" Johnson	Dylan & Cole Sprouse	Eli Manning
Hilary Duff	Jamie Lynn Spears	Jessie McCartney
Johnny Gruelle	Jonas Brothers	Jordin Sparks
LeBron James	Mia Hamm	Miley Cyrus
Miranda Cosgrove	Raven-Symone	Shaquille O'Neal
The Story of Harley-Davidson	Syd Hoff	Tiki Barber
Tom Brady	Tony Hawk	

Library of Congress Cataloging-in-Publication Data
Leavitt, Amie Jane.
 Miranda Cosgrove / by Amie Jane Leavitt.
     p. cm. — (A Robbie reader)
 Includes bibliographical references, filmography and index.
 ISBN 978-1-58415-720-5 (library bound)
 1. Cosgrove, Miranda, 1993– —Juvenile literature. 2. Actors—United States—
Biography—Juvenile literature. I. Title.
 PN2287.C634L43 2009
 791.4302'8092—dc22
 [B]
                                                                          2008008071

ABOUT THE AUTHOR: Amie Jane Leavitt is an accomplished author and photographer. She graduated from Brigham Young University as an education major and has since taught all subjects and grade levels in both private and public schools. She is an adventurer who loves to travel the globe in search of interesting story ideas and beautiful places to capture on film. She has written dozens of books for kids, including *Raven-Symone, Amanda Bynes,* and *Dylan and Cole Sprouse* for Mitchell Lane Publishers. Amie enjoys writing about people who work to achieve their dreams. For this reason, she particularly enjoyed researching and writing this book about Miranda Cosgrove.

PUBLISHER'S NOTE: The following story has been thoroughly researched and to the best of our knowledge represents a true story. While every possible effort has been made to ensure accuracy, the publisher will not assume liability for damages caused by inaccuracies in the data, and makes no warranty on the accuracy of the information contained herein. This story has not been authorized or endorsed by Miranda Cosgrove.

PLB

TABLE OF CONTENTS

Words in **bold** type can be found in the glossary.

Miranda has been in the acting business since she was a child. Over the years, she has worked really hard to improve her skills and talents onscreen. "Miranda has turned into this great actress," says Paul Kaplan, executive vice president of talent at Nickelodeon.

Her Very Own Show

September 8, 2007, was an important day for fourteen-year-old Miranda Cosgrove. On this day, *iCarly* **premiered** on Nickelodeon. New shows are aired all the time, but this was the first show in which Miranda was the star!

This premiere was actually two back-to-back episodes. The **network** ran it two days in a row. Over 13 million kids tuned in to watch it!

iCarly is kind of like a show within a show. Its about three teens who start their own web cast and become really successful at it. They also encourage viewers to send their own funny videos to the *iCarly* website. The show's main writer, Dan Schneider, knew kids would

Miranda loves spending time with the cast of *iCarly* (left to right): Jennette McCurdy, Dan Schneider, Jerry Trainor, Miranda, and Nathan Kress.

love this idea. "Kids want to be on, kids want to perform, and on a show like *iCarly* it's a perfect **venue** to showcase kids' talents," he said.

The viewers must have loved this idea, because over 300,000 kids visited icarly.com that first weekend. Thousands of kids sent in videos. "I'm sure we're going to get some people with some really great talent," Miranda said about the videos.

In *iCarly,* Miranda and her costars get to do a lot of crazy stunts. She and Jerry Trainor (Spencer) had fun with paint in a scene for the show.

The first **episode** featured kids who have unusual talents. One guy could shoot milk out of his eyes. Another one could speak backwards and make it sound natural. Miranda really liked a video about a clarinet-playing beat-boxer, sent in by a New York viewer. "It's like the coolest thing ever!" she told a reporter.

This wasn't the first time Miranda was on television. She had been in a number of movies and had just finished working on the popular series *Drake & Josh.* By the time she starred in *iCarly,* she was a pro.

Miranda was invited to attend many of the premieres for *The School of Rock*. She was the youngest cast member in that hit movie.

The Movie and Television Capital of the World

Miranda Taylor Cosgrove was born on May 14, 1993, in Los Angeles, California. Los Angeles— which includes Hollywood—is known as the movie and television capital of the world. At the time, Miranda's parents didn't realize that this was the perfect place for their daughter to be born.

Many kids dream of becoming a television or movie star. Yet when Miranda got into the business, she was far too young even to be dreaming about it. Miranda's break into stardom was accidental.

CHAPTER TWO

When Miranda was only three years old, she was at a restaurant with her parents. She was acting silly, dancing and singing by their table. A talent **agent** was sitting nearby. She thought the brown-eyed, brown-haired Miranda was a darling girl with a cute and interesting personality. Later, Miranda described the incident to a magazine reporter. "An agent asked [my parents] if I wanted to join her modeling and commercial agency. Of course, my mom went home and thought about it for a while, because she had never really thought about me getting into entertainment."

After thinking about it for a few weeks, Miranda's parents decided it would be all right for their daughter to at least try it out. They signed Miranda up with the talent agency. Just a short while later, when Miranda was four years old, she landed her first job. It was to advertise a citrus-flavored soft drink. "I did a Mello Yello commercial," she remembers. "And I was actually on the beach or something, so that's one of the first things I can remember doing."

Over the next few years, Miranda continued working small jobs. "I just kind of did

Miranda attended the 2008 Upfront Presentation in New York City with her mom, Chris Cosgrove. The presentation showed marketers new ways to advertise on Nickelodeon and other MTV Network channels.

commercials and modeling and stuff," she says. Then, when she started elementary school, she decided she wanted to do more. She began taking acting lessons after school. "When I was seven, I really realized that I loved doing it, and that's when I started trying out for more theatrical things . . . plays and stuff like that."

Miranda attended the 17th Annual Kids' Choice Awards in 2004.
Drake & Josh did not win that year, but it would bring home the
blimp for Best Television Show in 2006.

A Budding Young Star

When Miranda was eight years old, she tried out for a role on a show called *Drake & Josh.* The show's writers were hoping that Nickelodeon would want to run it as a **series**, so they looked for actors for the **pilot** episode. If the network liked the pilot, and enough people watched it, producers would agree to make the show a series.

This show would star two kids who had already been on Nickelodeon: Drake Bell and Josh Peck. They had been on *The Amanda Show,* starring Amanda Bynes. In *Drake & Josh,* they would be playing stepbrothers. Miranda tried out for the part of Drake's pesky little sister, Megan. There was a lot of competition for the part, but Miranda got it!

Miranda was excited about playing the part of Megan. For one, she finally got to have some **siblings**—even if they were just on television. In real life, Miranda is an only child. She was also excited about all the crazy things she would get to do on the show. Megan is the kind of kid who is perfect in front of her parents but then turns into a troublemaker when they are not around. She also does extreme things to her brothers. "Megan drives them crazy with her pranks. She even drenches them from head to toe with paint," Miranda said. In this way she is different from her character. "I'd never do anything like that," she said.

The cast worked together learning their lines and practicing their parts. They taped the show just before Miranda turned nine. In fact, she celebrated her birthday on the set!

After the pilot for *Drake & Josh* was finished, the cast had to wait to find out if Nickelodeon would run the show. In the meantime, Miranda flew to New York to be in her first movie: *The School of Rock,* starring Jack Black.

In the movie, Miranda plays the part of band manager Summer Hathaway—a serious child who is **obsessed** with getting straight As and being the teacher's pet. She had a lot of fun filming the movie. "We'd be laughing, and they'd say 'Cut!' and we'd think we did something wrong. And they put a lot of that in," she said.

Miranda enjoyed working with the other kids and also with the star of *The School of Rock.* "I really like Jack Black," she said. "He's awesome. . . . He's really funny in real life, but he's more laid back."

At the end of filming the movie, Miranda received some great news. Nickelodeon decided to run *Drake & Josh!* They would start taping the show as soon as she returned to Los Angeles.

The cast of *Drake & Josh* (left to right): Jonathan Goldstein, Nancy Sullivan, Drake Bell, Josh Peck, and Miranda Cosgrove. "It's just been so much fun getting to work with Drake and Josh," Miranda said. "I mean, they're like two of the funniest guys ever, and they make me laugh every day a million times."

The first episode of *Drake & Josh* aired on January 11, 2004. The show was a big hit, and it ran for three years. Miranda enjoyed working with the cast, and they became good friends offscreen too.

During the *Drake & Josh* years, Miranda also made guest appearances on other Nick shows, such as *Zoey 101, Unfabulous,* and *Just Jordan.* She also **auditioned** for movies. In 2005, she played the part of Joni North in the movie *Yours, Mine and Ours.* In this film, Miranda would have seventeen onscreen siblings! Just as in *Drake & Josh,* Drake Bell played one of her brothers. She also made good friends with actors Haley Ramm and Miki Ishikawa, who played her sisters.

Also in 2005, Miranda was the voice of Munch in the movie *Here Comes Peter Cottontail.* The next year she played the role of Hanna Mills in the movie *The Wild Stallion* and the role of Karen Sussman in *Keeping Up with the Steins.* About her role in *The Wild Stallion,* Miranda said, "We did it in Utah and it was really pretty there. We got to race [horses] and do all this really cool stuff."

"[Miranda is] a beautiful girl with amazing features—a doll to look at," says Dan Schneider, producer of *iCarly*.

CHAPTER FOUR

iCarly

While Miranda was on Nickelodeon, she worked a lot with writer Dan Schneider. He had been responsible for many of the successful shows on the network, including *All That, The Amanda Show,* and *Drake & Josh.* Schneider thought Miranda was a very talented actress.

One night while watching some funny videos on YouTube, Schneider came up with an idea for another television show. He immediately thought of Miranda. "She's a star," he told a reporter in 2007. "She is one of the classiest little girls that I've ever met. I don't believe I've ever heard her complain about anything, I don't think I've seen her in a bad mood once in my life, and I've done 61 episodes of television with her. . . . Miranda's the real deal; there's nothing Hollywood about her."

This new show, *iCarly,* would be about three friends who post one of their funny videos online. Kids who watch it think it's hilarious. The three become instantly popular in the online community. They decide to start their own web show and encourage kids to send in videos of their own. Schneider was very excited about his idea, because nothing like it had ever been done before.

He approached Miranda about the idea. "When I first heard about [it], I thought it was so cool. If I were at home and watching TV, I'd want to send in a video," she said.

Miranda agreed to play the part of the main character, Carly Shay. Jennette McCurdy and Nathan Kress would play

Carly's two best friends, Sam and Freddy. Carly and Sam host the weekly web show, and Freddy is in charge of the technical side and camera work.

From the start, *iCarly* was a big success. Miranda likes the show because it allows kids across the country to get involved. "It's really the first show for teens that has a great reality element to it," she says. "I think the cool part for me is seeing all the kids' videos."

She also likes to spend time with her new costars. Jennette and Miranda have become good friends. Jennette says, "We have a ton of fun. We have these little handshakes that we think of and we'll sing songs and make music videos for the songs that we like and we have a great time in school. It's just such a great experience."

Schneider is happy he chose Miranda as the lead. He believes Miranda will be an "extremely sought after actress" in the future.

Miranda has become a popular actress—so she has had to deal with plenty of gossip. Some people thought she and *iCarly* costar Nathan Kress were an item, but Miranda says, "Nathan has a crush on me on the show, but in real life we're like best friends."

A Regular Girl

Miranda may be a big star both on television and in movies, but in real life, she's just a regular girl. One of her favorite things to do is go to the movies. "I'm a movie junkie," she told a reporter in 2006. "We have a Friday night movie thing, everybody from *Drake & Josh* meets and we go see a movie."

Along with her cast mates, Miranda is also good friends with kids she met in elementary school, and with some neighborhood kids. "My next-door neighbor is my age, and she's a crack up, and I hang out with her all the time."

Besides hanging out with her friends, Miranda enjoys music and sports. She plays the electric guitar and the piano, and she sings. She also took a few saxophone lessons for her role in *Yours, Mine and Ours.* She sings the theme song for *iCarly.*

She was introduced to her favorite sport, horseback riding, by one of her friends. Miranda says, "[My friend] went all the time, and I thought it was really cool, and I was always jealous, because, who doesn't love horses? So one day she actually asked me to go with her, so I went, and I've been taking lessons, and doing it ever since."

Another one of Miranda's favorite activities is fencing, a type of sword-fighting. Fencing is an Olympic sport. Although Miranda probably doesn't have dreams of competing on that level, she still enjoys learning more about her new hobby. "I thought it would be like *Pirates of the Caribbean* with all the sword fights, but it's actually really hard. You work a lot of muscles, and it takes a lot of upper-body strength," she commented.

Miranda attended regular school until her schedule became so demanding that she started homeschooling. This is typical of how child actors learn their school lessons. In 2006, she started taking classes through an online high school. At first it felt strange to go to school this way, but soon she got used to it and even grew to like the program. The kids in the program were able to get together for different activities. Miranda told a reporter in 2006, "You go and you get to meet kids and like, take classes, which is really cool. . . . You get to meet new people and kids your age."

Miranda enjoys school and has big plans for her future. "I definitely want to go to college. That's a big thing with me. I have a few friends, that we're like, already planning, and we want to go to the same college, which would be really fun. I don't know. I'd love to be an actor, but I'd also like to be a marine biologist. I'm really into the sea."

Until then, Miranda is just enjoying her life. She loves her job, and she especially enjoys her fans. She's always excited when kids recognize her when she's out in public. She's grateful for their support.

In October 2007, Miranda attended Camp Ronald McDonald's Halloween Carnival. This event is held every year and lets kids with cancer have a fun time with their families. Miranda mingled with the kids and families, and she signed autographs.

Miranda likes to help others, too. In 2005, she participated in Nickelodeon's Let's Just Play—Go Healthy Challenge. This was a program designed to help kids get off the couch and get out and play. Miranda said, "It's important for kids today to be aware of the health risks of eating a lot of junk food and not being active enough. I play tennis, fence, and ride my bike, but I know I could be doing more." She said that the kids who participated in the program really inspired her. After working with them, she wanted to help get more kids involved in a healthy lifestyle.

Miranda knows that many kids dream of becoming big stars. Her advice for them? "Just keep trying and never give up. . . . A lot of people go to one audition, and they think they're going to get [a part] right away, and then when they don't, they feel bad. But it's really no big deal. Most people have to try and try, so just keep trying, and work at it, and you'll eventually get it." And if Miranda—a regular girl who likes to do kid stuff just like you—can live her dreams, then you most certainly can too!

CHRONOLOGY

1993 Miranda Taylor Cosgrove is born on May 14 in Los Angeles.

1996 Miranda is discovered by a talent agency.

1997 She makes her debut in a Mello Yello television commercial.

2000 Miranda begins taking acting lessons after school.

2001 She tries out for a role on the Nickelodeon show *Drake & Josh* and gets it.

2002 Miranda celebrates her ninth birthday on the set of *Drake & Josh* following the taping of the show's pilot episode. She flies to New York to work in her first film, *The School of Rock,* starring Jack Black.

2004 The first episode of *Drake & Josh* is aired on Nickelodeon on January 11. The show is a big success and lasts for three years.

2005 Miranda plays Joni North in her second film, *Yours, Mine and Ours.* She is the voice of Munch in the film *Here Comes Peter Cottontail.* She participates in Nickelodeon's Let's Just Play—Go Healthy Challenge.

2006 Miranda plays the role of Hanna Mills in the film *The Wild Stallion* and the role of Karen Sussman in *Keeping Up with the Steins.* She begins taking classes through an online high school.

2007 Miranda plays the lead role on *iCarly,* which premieres on September 8. She attends Camp Ronald McDonald's Halloween Carnival for families in October.

2008 Miranda stars alongside Drake Bell and Josh Peck in the film *Drake & Josh in New York!* Miranda signs a recording contract with Columbia Records.

FILMOGRAPHY

2008 *Drake & Josh in New York!*

2007 *iCarly* (TV)

2006 *Keeping Up with the Steins*

The Wild Stallion

2005 *Yours, Mine and Ours*

Here Comes Peter Cottontail: The Movie (voice)

2004 *Drake & Josh* (TV)

2003 *The School of Rock*

FIND OUT MORE

Books

While there are no other books about Miranda Cosgrove, you might enjoy these other biographies from Mitchell Lane Publishers.

Leavitt, Amie Jane. *Amanda Bynes.* Hockessin, Delaware: Mitchell Lane Publishers, 2008.

Leavitt, Amie Jane. *Dylan and Cole Sprouse.* Hockessin, Delaware: Mitchell Lane Publishers, 2008.

Mattern, Joanne. *Drake Bell and Josh Peck.* Hockessin, Delaware: Mitchell Lane Publishers, 2008.

Works Consulted

Campbell, Janis. "Get Interactive with the Interesting *iCarly.*" *Detroit Free Press,* September 20, 2007. http://www.accessmylibrary.com/coms2/summary_0286-32926171_ITM

Dee, Jonathan. "Tween on the Screen." *New York Times,* April 8, 2007. http://www.nytimes.com/2007/04/08/magazine/08NICKELODEON.t.html?_r=1&pagewanted=print&oref=slogin

DeLeon, Kris. "*iCarly* Premiere Draws 13 Million Viewers." *Buddy TV,* September 13, 2007. http://www.buddytv.com/articles/drake-and-josh/icarly-premiere-draws-13-milli-10782.aspx

Keveney, Bill. "Nickelodeon Fuses TV and Internet, Seeks Users' Video." *USA Today,* September 4, 2007, page 10B. http://www.usatoday.com/printedition/life/20070904/d_icarly04.art.htm

FIND OUT MORE

Kinon, Christina. " 'Carly' Star & Miranda Cosgrove Have Lots in Common." *New York Daily News,* September 15, 2007. http://www.nydailynews. com/entertainment/tv/2007/09/15/2007-09-15_carly__star_miranda_ cosgrove_have_lots_i.html

Larsen, Peter. "Nickelodeon Show 'iCarly' Seeks a Link with Young Fans." *The Orange County Register.* http://www.ocregister.com/ocregister/ entertainment/television/features/article_1839809.php

Miller, Gerry. "Yours, Mine, and Ours." *Scholastic.* http://teacher.scholastic. com/scholasticnews/indepth/yours_mine_ours_interviews.asp

"Miranda Cosgrove." *The Star Scoop.* http://www.thestarscoop.com/2006dec/miranda-cosgrove.php

Moore, Scott. "Teen Actress Sees 'iCarly' as Welcome Departure." [Wilmington, Delaware] *News Journal.* Accessed January 2008. http://www.delawareonline.com/apps/pbcs.dll/article?AID=/20071109/ LIFE/711090304/1005/LIFE

Morreale, Marie. "A Talk with Jennette McCurdy." *Scholastic News.* October 19, 2007. http://www2.scholastic.com/browse/article.jsp?id=3748275

Morreale, Marie. "Chatting with Miranda Cosgrove." *Scholastic News.* September 19, 2007. http://www2.scholastic.com/browse/article.jsp?id=3748270

"Nickelodeon Tween Stars Miranda Cosgrove . . ." *PR Newswire,* June 14, 2007. http://www.accessmylibrary.com/coms2/summary_0286-31263572_ITM

Rizzo, Monica. "Meet TV's New Tween Stars." *People.* October 22, 2007, Vol 68, Issue 17, page 44.

Rogers, John. " 'iCarly' Combines the Internet with TV." September 18, 2007. http://abcnews.go.com/Entertainment/wireStory?id=3619200

Smith, Lynn. "A High-Amped 'School'." http://www.jsonline.com/story/ index.asp?id=173465

Stransky, Tanner. "Miranda Cosgrove: Teen Player." *Entertainment Weekly,* October 11, 2007, http://www.ew.com/ew/article/0,,20152065,00.html

On the Internet

Jennette McCurdy—Official Site http://www.jennettemccurdy.com/

Nickelodeon: Meet the Casts, Miranda Cosgrove. http://www.nick.com/all_ nick/tv_supersites/cast.jhtml?show_id=dra&cast=Miranda%20Cosgrove

"Q and A with Miranda Cosgrove." *Know Your World Extra; Weekly Reader* http://www.accessmylibrary.com/coms

GLOSSARY

agent (AY-jint)—A person who searches for talented individuals to hire for acting or modeling jobs.

audition (aw-DIH-shun)—Try out for a job.

episode (EH-pih-sohd)—A single show in a television series.

network—A company that produces and airs television shows.

obsessed (ob-SESD)—Thinking only about one subject.

pilot (PY-lit)—The first episode of a show taped in order to convince a network to adopt the show as a series.

premiered (preh-MEERD)—Shown for the first time.

series (SEE-rees)—A chain of episodes.

sibling—A brother or sister.

venue (VEN-yoo)—The place where an event can be seen.

INDEX